T0082678

POCKET
YOUR PERSONAL ECONOMY

Amr Muneer Dahab

authorHOUSE

AuthorHouse™
1663 Liberty Drive
Bloomington, IN 47403
www.authorhouse.com
Phone: 833-262-8899

© 2021 Amr Muneer Dahab. All rights reserved.

No part of this book may be reproduced, stored in a retrieval system, or
transmitted by any means without the written permission of the author.

Published by AuthorHouse 09/15/2021

ISBN: 978-1-6655-3828-2 (sc)
ISBN: 978-1-6655-3829-9 (e)

Print information available on the last page.

Any people depicted in stock imagery provided by Getty Images are models,
and such images are being used for illustrative purposes only.
Certain stock imagery © Getty Images.

This book is printed on acid-free paper.

Because of the dynamic nature of the Internet, any web addresses or links contained in
this book may have changed since publication and may no longer be valid. The views
expressed in this work are solely those of the author and do not necessarily reflect the
views of the publisher, and the publisher hereby disclaims any responsibility for them.

To everyone who is trying to control their budget in vain.

CONTENTS

Preface ix

If You Are Spendthrift by Nature 1
If You Are Miserly by Nature 4
In the Mall 7
On Vacation 10
The Best Investment 13
Employee and Businessman 16
Professional Consultation versus Traditional Advice 19
Budget Control 23
Virtual Financial World 26
When Your Finances Run Low 29
When Your Income Increases 33
Your Debts 36
Your References in Spending and Saving 39
Taking Risk 42
Your Retirement Plan 45
Your Wish List 48
What Does a Blessing Mean? 51
Money and Happiness 53

PREFACE

The people most able to give financial advice to others are not always those who have received academic training or those who have great saving abilities and organizing skills. Sometimes the most troubled person in their financial affairs may be able to determine exactly what a wasteful person should do to get their finances right, even if the person who advises is not able to apply their advice to themselves.

I do not at all claim to be a financially disciplined person, nor do I, in return, think I am remarkably extravagant. Nevertheless, what I can say with confidence is that I am attentive to my spending problems and to what I must always do to rectify my finances, even if I am not always able to bring my plans accurately into reality.

I hope that reading *Pocket* will help you to better understand and deal with your financial reality, regardless of whether you are a spendthrift or a frugal person. The challenges of money lie not only in controlling overspending but also in getting rid of the obsession with thrift.

IF YOU ARE SPENDTHRIFT BY NATURE

($) Spendthrift people are creative in inventing ways to spend money. If you are unable to completely control your spending, at least try to invent ways to spend as an investment that will bring you a constant or even immediate return.

($) A wasteful person cannot be confident in controlling their spending, no matter how many consultations they receive and harsh practical experiences they go through. Force yourself to invest or save with a mandatory deduction from your monthly income in exchange for a loan, for example, that you utilize to purchase a fixed asset—like a house—or start any project that brings you a reasonable fixed income.

($) Don't give up on trying, no matter how impossible the task seems to you. It is better to constantly try to rationalize your spending, even though you would probably fail so many times and succeed only a few times, than to let your financial problems escalate and lead to a catastrophic end.

If you do not need a larger size or more quantity, do not fall into the trap of buying a bigger capacity in discount offers just assuming that saves money. The larger volume may be an obstacle when storing it, and the extra quantity might lead to the consequences of excessive consumption.

The situation that prompts you to review your spending drastically is not only when you feel that you are on the verge of declaring bankruptcy. Budget review and continuous spending control are necessary for every person, but a wasteful person needs to review their budget and their spending mindset much more than the average person.

Minimize as much as possible asking for financial aid from those close to you. Instead, do not hesitate to seek precious advice from those who are trustworthy and have valued knowledge and experience.

It is not wise to wait for a sudden increase in your income to cover a fixed monthly deficit in your budget. Take immediate remedial action to reduce your expenses by eliminating the least important items from your monthly purchase list.

The satisfactory budget consumption is not necessarily proportional to the amount of your income. However, to best control and be satisfied with your budget if you are spendthrift, you must compress your expenses until they become obviously less than your income, no matter how much that income is.

💰 Don't buy everything you want at once. Consider the principle of deferring the purchase of nonessential items and distributing them throughout the year, or even longer than that, to allow your budget to accommodate your desires comfortably.

💰 Don't despair when you find your urge to buy irresistible. If you can never give up thinking about some purchases that you find urgent but beyond your monthly means, instead of borrowing, substitute some items on your regular shopping list and buy what is urgent or even what you just feel a strong desire to own.

IF YOU ARE MISERLY BY NATURE

2

💰 Continuing to save nonstop and with the least amount of spending means eventually you will leave your money to someone else when you pass away. Like donating blood, generous spending on yourself and others from time to time breathes life into your money, refreshes it, and makes you feel its benefit without necessarily losing any noticeable amount.

💰 It is good to have the ability to save, and it is better to be good at investing. The most important thing is to know how to enjoy what you save and invest.

💰 There are some social and public life obligations that you have to fulfill, no matter how keen you are to collect money, but in general, being a lover of money and careful in spending is a personal matter. However, it is prudent if others' attention could be dragged more to your spending and charitable deeds than to your love of money and your eagerness to save.

While people who are more adept at saving are role models for miserly persons, there are more important sources of inspiration for miserly persons—to benefit from them deeply at different levels—in those who do not skimp on their money but use it prudently and wisely.

It's OK to buy a high-end brand item if you can afford it without overburdening your budget. If you decide to stand out, it will no longer make sense to feel resented about the exaggerated price of an item because you think it is too much for the cost.

The definitions of *miserliness* and *generosity* are constantly changing based on time, place, and the nature of life in general. Eventually, it is your money. The important thing is to achieve the balance that satisfies you between the necessity of saving—for any future investment or to face the surprises of time in general—and meeting the innate need for rational spending to bring yourself pleasure and comfort.

No problem if you find your sheer pleasure mainly in hoarding money. You just have to be aware of the consequences for you socially—and psychologically in the long run—and be able to face those consequences with confidence.

The most valuable act of charity is that which you undertake not for the sake of ostentation or the pursuit of an indirect interest. However, to spend your money on charitable causes that aim behind it for some material interests—in one way or another—is better in any case than abstaining completely from spending on charitable work.

Not as a challenge to deny the accusation of miserliness, but you can still please others with symbolic gifts that are not necessarily expensive but are carefully selected.

Do not be ashamed of your extreme love for money if others confront you about it, and at the same time, do not flaunt it. It is important to accept yourself as you are, constantly trying to improve what you see necessary and possible for improvement. On the other hand, others should accept you for who you are as long as the manifestations of your qualities—even those that greatly annoy them—do not infringe on their affairs.

IN THE MALL

3

$ The mall and the markets in general are primarily places to buy and not for wandering and entertainment. If you just feel upset and do not want to buy any items, it is better to go somewhere else for a walk or to relax.

$ Don't let the exhibits write your shopping list. Get the list done before you head out to the mall.

$ Try to get done not only your shopping list but even your shops list as much as you can before you head out to the market.

$ Keep your shopping list accurate, and stick to it. But it's important to remember to take into account a safety margin for additional expenditures against any surprises, such as an unexpected increase in the price of an item, having to replace an unavailable item with a more expensive one, or even any emergency addition to the list.

After preparing your shopping list and going to the market, if you were surprised by an item that you could not resist or discovered that you needed it very much and it was not available before but it is exceeding all your current budget preparations, work seriously to delete the least needed items or what you can postpone in your shopping list.

There is no single store or even one mall that is the best in everything, whether in terms of the quality and variety of goods offered or their prices. The market is large, and the shops are changing and being renewed; therefore, carefully select your stores list and continuously update it to suit your renewed needs and the changes that occur to the market itself.

Sale season is only a good opportunity to buy the discounted items that you've been wanting to buy. Beware of rushing to buy items, no matter how tempting the discount is, unless you really need them. Don't let sale season dictate what to buy just because items become more affordable.

You don't have to pay more for an item just because of the exorbitant rent of the shop. You might be able to buy the same item from a simple shop in a modest place.

In the world of shopping, there is no such concept as "loyalty" in the traditional sense. Give your shopping loyalty to the stores that give you the best privileges, not necessarily to the ones that offer you a clever shopping trick called "the loyalty card."

Remember that the privileges are not just limited to the low prices but also include other essential needs related to purchasing, such as after-sales service and long-term store's reliability.

ON VACATION

4

$ Without good, advance, dedicated budget planning, the vacation may become a burden to you rather than a source of recreation and happiness.

$ You most probably won't have a problem budgeting precisely for your vacation and spending accordingly if you plan and control the budget for the rest of the year satisfactorily.

$ Vacations are usually skilled at stealing the keys to the spending doors that you used to control throughout the previous months of the year. Prepare for the vacation with a sharp plan, make sure to implement it accurately, and do not leave things for the unlimited temptations and surprises of the vacation.

$ The vacation budget is necessarily different from the budget for the rest of the year. It's not just about spending more or spending less as much as it is an account set aside to meet the vacation requirements you have planned.

💰 Do not be satisfied by just observing and adjusting your budget in the face of increasing vacation expenses. Use the vacation itself as an opportunity to reflect on and enhance your overall budget. In addition to evaluating how to minimize or even eliminate some expenses, you can achieve that enhancement by trying to get inspired on new resources to increase your income.

💰 Lots of vacation recreation requires some money, but you can still have pleasant times while on vacation without spending money more than usual. Having a quality time, no matter how long it takes, with loved ones from family and friends in novel activities will bring you priceless psychological and spiritual benefits.

💰 Plan your vacation budget in a balanced way. Do not make all your concern to barely overcome the vacation budget experience by spending the last cent in the last hour of the last day of the vacation and waiting eagerly for the first salary after returning to work.

💰 Unless you have a clear investment earmarked for it, deal with the vacation's advance salary as if it hadn't been credited to your account.

If you are spending your vacation far from your country or workplace, and you have had a rare opportunity to buy or invest and have thought of borrowing, that is fine. However, it is wise to think carefully about the feasibility of that opportunity and ensure your ability to pay off the debt on time.

According to the vacation program, you may have to complete your purchases during a specific period, which may be at the beginning of the vacation. That's OK, but try as much as you can to spread your shopping experience and enjoy it throughout the holiday so that you don't feel frustrated or empty in the middle of it.

THE BEST INVESTMENT

5

No single investment is the best. The optimal types of investment depend not only on your resources, tendencies, and capabilities but also on your age and on your previous experiences in investing and life in general.

How you spend is the basis and the reflection of how much you save. Spending and saving are two complementary processes, each of which leads to the results of the other. A thoughtful balance between spending and saving is the beginning of the road to good investment.

Your investment does not mean that you wait while you save an amount of money and then see what you can do with it. Sometimes waiting misses a rare opportunity. If you can deduct a significant part of your monthly income as a fixed contribution to a well-thought-out investment, it is not necessary to postpone the opportunity waiting greedily for a great investment you dream of.

A better investment is closely related to the culture of the place. It's OK to deviate from the ordinary sometimes, but slow down and think carefully before knocking on the door of an unfamiliar investment.

Investing within a heavily popular field is just as risky as investing in a new one. With the widespread investment, there is the risk of market saturation, and with the new investment, there are no previous experiences that you can benefit from their lessons. Each case has its risks, which should be carefully considered before deciding to start.

The most important thing to avoid when deciding on any investment is overconfidence and extreme hesitation alike. Study your project carefully, and consult more than one whom you trust for their experience and honesty, and take your decision after that. Do not forget the necessity of monitoring, auditing, and updating throughout the investment period.

Do not hesitate to take the decision to withdraw from the investment whenever it becomes clear to you that things are not going in the right direction. If necessary, sacrifice some money in the middle of the road to avoid further losses.

$ It is OK to be taken in by the splendor of a great investment that brought huge profits to its owner, but what suits you may be another investment that is less glamorous. Look at all the business around you and choose what suits your abilities. Encourage yourself to advance your ambitions, but not only by chasing after not-well-thought-out aspirations of great and quick wealth.

$ With the right choice, sincerity, patience, and love of your work, you can turn a similar project that brought another person an average revenue into a huge project with great profits.

$ Eventually, you are the only person who has to decide which investment is best suited to you, no matter how much advice you hear from others, including trustworthy confidants and competent professionals.

EMPLOYEE AND BUSINESSMAN

6

The main difference between the employee and the businessman is that the former expects a fixed salary at the end of the month while the latter looks forward to deals with open returns at every hour of the day, and the behavior of each in spending is based on these two facts.

There is nothing wrong if an employee decided to take a businessman as a role model in any financial aspect except for purchases, even if only in some aspects of spending. The employee should postpone this step until they completely move from the group of employees to the category of businessmen.

There are businessmen who behave like employees, not only in the way they spend but also in managing their business. A businessman of such behavior can be viewed as an employee with a high fixed income.

💰 Practically, it is rare for a person to start their life as a businessman unless they work with their family or inherited the business from them. Some may remain in the framework of the job while trying to stumble for many years before they independently manage their own business. In any case, running a business is just like a talent that needs to be allowed to flourish. Although the one who is primarily responsible for extracting opportunities for talent is the talent owner themselves, luck/fate has the greatest role in determining the time for the talent to explode with success in its own world.

💰 The businessman is not necessarily smarter in general than the employee is, but they are talented in the field that brings money, and money in turn brings everything, let alone the intangible concepts that are relative, discretionary, and equally often confounding before everyone.

💰 If you're missing out on business talent, studying won't make the talent. Serious study and perseverance will not make you an entrepreneur but will only give you the possibility to run businesses, including the one you own.

💰 Like other fields, in business, it is not a matter of talent versus lack of talent. The talents themselves range from weak to medium to great to exceptional.

You don't need to be a businessman to live comfortably. Through ambition and perseverance, you can live a fulfilling life by moving up the career ladder to the highest positions. It comes down to the career field you choose, and ultimately what matters is not your title at work as much as what you accomplish and achieve through it.

If you are an employee, it is natural for you to have your dreams and aspirations to get rich. It's OK to try your luck in business and risk once, twice, and three times in the beginning, but make sure that what you have is a true passion that does not lack talent and not just rosy dreams of getting rich. Note that the important thing is not necessarily to move from the group of employees to the category of prominent businessmen. What you need to succeed may be to carefully choose the nature and size of the project that is appropriate for your capabilities and not to soar in the space of abstract dreams of wealth.

A proactive employee does not need the title of a "businessman" to open a small business or practice a simple commercial activity that will generate further income for them in addition to their job.

PROFESSIONAL CONSULTATION VERSUS TRADITIONAL ADVICE

7

There is no fundamental conflict between both of them. Traditional advice is based on life experience related to what humans have gone through, and professional consultations are based on a scientific vision to ensure the best practical results based on what could be deduced from the same experiences. The conflict that may arise between traditional advice and professional consultation is in fact possible between two pieces of traditional advice or between two professional consultations. In any case, there is no single definitive opinion regarding any financial issue, similar to all aspects of life.

Whatever the style of advice or consultation you prefer and the experience of those who give it to you, you are the only one who is able to extract what suits you and how to apply it on the ground.

💰 Do not underestimate advice in the most complex financial matters when you receive it spontaneously from a simple person. Consider that advice carefully, as it may be your way out of the problem. At times, the solution to the most complex problems—even the technical ones—involves insight, which requires primarily a calm spirit to unfold before it.

💰 Financial management books and specialized training courses are not everything. It is good to take the initiative to read a specialized book and enroll in a financial training course, but it is important to continue reading and training. The most important is to work hard to link everything you receive from books and courses to reality and strive to apply that to your financial affairs, extracting every time the lessons learned for further enhancement.

💰 In mathematical equations, you get the result according to your accuracy in dealing with the correct numbers and different coefficients and variables, but it is important that you primarily use the appropriate equation. In financial issues, the matter is a little bit complicated. The challenge is often away from choosing an equation or calculating accurately; it lies mainly in your financial insight and your determination to implement your decisions more than being related to the financial approach you choose.

Sometimes when a patient despairs after trying all advanced medical techniques to follow up on their condition, they resort to some forms of traditional medicine to treat their condition. You do not necessarily have to deal with traditional financial advice in the same way; on the contrary, it is better to consider available traditional advice in parallel as you are looking for or studying the results of professional advice.

In some situations there is a conflict between traditional advice and professional consultation, but this conflict is not the norm. Even when we encounter such a clear contradiction, each specific situation determines the outcome in favor of either direction prevails, and that determination depends largely on the nature of the situation and its context in time and place.

It is always important to pay attention to the use of the appropriate means of assistance, depending on the situation and what surrounds it in time and place. Even in very serious self-defense situations, for instance, it makes no sense to use a firearm if brandishing a cold weapon is enough to keep you out of danger.

$ It would be best if the professional financial consultant themselves had a deep belief in the value of traditional advice toward financial enlightenment and inspiration.

$ Over time, the gist of each deep professional financial nugget of advice turns in one way or another into traditional advice and aphorisms.

BUDGET CONTROL

8

$ It's best to stick to a regular spending plan that covers everything, including your rewards to yourself for any achievement and any incidentals in general.

$ No matter how careful you are by nature and diligently controlling your spending, you will find yourself from time to time facing sharp turns that take you outside your plan, including what you dedicated for emergency expenses. Do not panic and try to steady as quickly as possible, whether with austerity measures or by a disciplined withdrawal of your savings just as needed. There will come a time—sooner or later—when you will get back what you lost as long as you haven't floundered through your financial critical juncture.

$ No personal or family budget, or even the budget of an institution or a state, is always staunch. The challenges of any budget often arise from emergency spending requirements, no matter how carefully we calculate them. An emergency does not become an emergency if we can fully and accurately anticipate it.

You don't have to be a financial expert to control your budget. Budget control at the personal levels requires more talent and applied skills than complex theoretical knowledge.

Budget control does not mean spending less but maintaining the spending plan even if the planned spending is huge.

The challenge of budget control lies primarily in rational spending, not just in abstaining from unplanned and unnecessary spending.

Like the budget of any official institution, your own budget needs constant periodic reviews and sometimes immediate serious interventions to adjust it in order to prevent a critical deficit.

A collapsed budget needs more attention to control it than your budget in normal situations does. Do not let your preoccupation with the search for an urgent remedy for the collapsed budget keep you from carefully controlling the available amount, as this may lead to further collapse, which in turn makes the treatment more complicated.

It is good to come out at the end of the month or the end of the year with a budget surplus, but it is important that this surplus did not come at the expense of a frozen investment that could have been achieved utilizing the surplus if the budget was calculated at the beginning more accurately. In all cases, the lesson learned should be considered to benefit from it in the next budget.

Lessons learned from your previous budget control experiences will be more useful if you carefully contemplate them not only to avoid past mistakes, but also to anticipate potential challenges and try to avoid them.

VIRTUAL FINANCIAL WORLD

9

The facilities of virtual financial worlds often encourage you to spend more than they might help you to save. Whatever it is, the tendency to spend or save is a personal nature rather than being linked to surrounding circumstances. The important thing is that you take advantage of the facilities of the virtual financial worlds—regardless of the intention to spend or to save—so that managing your financial affairs becomes easier and more organized.

The virtual financial world is no longer an option; it is part of today's world that is about to be virtual in most of its aspects. Do not hesitate to take the initiative to knock on the doors of virtual management of your financial affairs, even if it is possible to continue managing your finances through traditional nonvirtual channels.

It is just the management style that is virtual while the money we deal with is naturally real. The question that is not related only to money but at all levels is this: is it wise to call something "virtual" just because we don't touch it with our hands?

💰 Eventually, your prowess in dealing with money, not your computer skills and technological capabilities, is what will primarily make you succeed in the virtual financial worlds.

💰 The virtual financial world created many new concepts in transactions and financial management, but in the end, none of these concepts changed anything within the essence of money.

💰 The tech geniuses of the virtual financial worlds are still working for businessmen.

💰 The challenge facing a businessman who still insists on dealing through traditional means comes from customers from the public before being from competitors among businessmen or from official institutions that manage financial affairs.

💰 If a businessman wants to break through and sweep today's markets, he must understand the new dimensions and renewable rules of business across virtual worlds and not necessarily delve into the concept of the virtual world itself or the subtleties of its technology.

A genuine businessman knows how to adapt every traditional business to develop its idea through the virtual business world and not only being satisfied with making it possible to sell through electronic purchase sites by credit card.

An open-minded entrepreneur is not afraid of any new idea in the business world and never slows down to keep up with such ideas. On the contrary, they view revolutionary ideas as valuable opportunities to develop their business, and they take the initiative to invent some of them.

WHEN YOUR FINANCES RUN LOW

10

When your financial resources begin to decline, you should immediately start reducing your spending or saving, whichever is less priority for you.

Finding an additional source of income to compensate for the shortfall in your resources will help you restore your regular status and psychological balance. But do not rush to engage in ill-thought-out activities, and at the same time, do not hesitate to engage in any secured sideline work if you get the chance, even if it is somewhat less than your ambitions.

It is important to keep your spending priorities always set ready, so that choosing what to give up—when your financial resources decline—does not become a confusing challenge for you.

The austerity measures that you follow when your financial resources are low may be upsetting, but try to use it as a good opportunity to discover the excessive spending behavior that you can get rid of even after your financial resources return to what they were. On the other hand, it is OK to pamper yourself with what you see fit when things settle down and you return to your previous financial situation. In any case, the difference between what is necessary and what is superfluous remains relative to a far extent and depends largely on your financial situation and the circumstances surrounding you.

In times of acute crisis involving society as a whole, or even the whole world, there is a somewhat different challenge to the austerity behavior that most people find themselves compelled to follow. The paradox is that the behavior of society—after the end of the crisis and the return of economic life to normal—is similar to the behavior of separate individuals after the end of a financial crisis that each one of them had gone through at a certain time, which means that the behavior of societies is almost actually the arithmetic mean of the behavior of separate individuals.

Proactive action is, of course, more effective. It is important to look at the short, medium, or even long term and try to foresee the probabilities of any decrease in any of your financial resources. This will help you adjust your budget while you are in a comfortable position and make the relevant decision whenever needed in a calmer, wiser, and more prudent manner.

It is useful to review your spending and study the possibilities of reducing in some respects without there being any necessity or indications of a potential decrease in your financial resources over any coming period. Such evaluations are important not only to study the possibilities of reducing expenditures but mainly to redistribute expenditures, helping to update your budget and refresh your financial affairs. This may include adding what is reduced in some respects to an increase due in others.

When you decide to take austerity measures to counter a decline in your finances, do not rush to imitate anyone you know in a similar situation. Austerity measures are many and varied in forms; to ensure their effectiveness, you must choose from them not only what suits your budget but what better matches your nature as well.

It is better to have more than one austerity measure to choose from in the beginning, as well as for the sake of replacing one plan with another in the event of failure to continue what you started with after a while.

Austerity measures' period to confront the decline in your financial resources does not mean that you should undergo continuous suffering until you regain your previous financial position. Take this forced opportunity to discover the special pleasure inherent in some simple living experiences in food, clothing, and transportation—and most importantly the advantages inherent in the human relationships that the experience allows you through communication with new categories of people.

WHEN YOUR INCOME INCREASES

11

When your financial resources increase, the doors of spending will open widely before you. It is neither wise nor logical to deprive yourself of what you wished to have or enjoy when your resources were limited. It is important to set your new budget to accommodate the new spending doors that have opened before you without forgetting the amount you need to save.

Future investments and emergency spending requirements, which you are saving for, are directly proportional to the size of your financial resources. Accordingly, the more your financial resources and the higher your spending pattern, the more you need to save.

With the increase in your sources of income, allocate funds for charitable work or increase them if you are already used to spending on charitable work. This will benefit you in achieving a psychological balance between the material and morals in your life that you desperately need, in addition to the impact on consolidating your honorable social presence as a result of the announced part of charitable work.

$ It is wise not to put off your happiness waiting for it to come true with an increase in your finances. Money may make you more comfortable in material aspects, but happiness—whatever it means—is not associated with money necessarily in a direct or inverse proportion.

$ It is natural and important that the effect of your increasing financial resources appears on you, but stay as far as possible from bragging, and beware even of unintentional ostentation. Provoking others will do you no good, whether those whose resources are still limited or those with high incomes who see you as a new guest to their community.

$ Managing your financial resources becomes more difficult as these resources increase, especially if they become very diversified. This requires more attention and caution so that this increase does not become a heavy burden instead of a blessing that brings comfort.

$ When your financial resources increase significantly, this often leads you to the necessity of dealing with new social classes. Do not be afraid to approach these categories, and do not rush toward them at the same time. In any case, the situation does not require you to abandon your old social group and enter a new one, but you must—for many ethical and even practical considerations—remain closely related and loyal to the social group from which you ascended.

When your financial resources increase, continuing to increase the number of these resources or even maintaining it should not remain an obsession; the most important thing is the continuation of the feasibility of these resources as a source of rewarding income. Be vigilant to maintain the usefulness and vitality of these resources, even if this requires getting rid of some of them—when their management problems worsen—to allow an opportunity to focus on the rest of the most effective resources.

It is important to pay attention to the time when you realize that you are in a better financial position. Feeling rich is not always related to additional sources of income or wealth that suddenly falls on you from the sky. You may achieve your target getting rich when your savings are enough to stop your obsession with collecting money and to start enjoying it.

Some items will remain difficult for you to purchase even after you become richer. Even on a purely financial level, you will not necessarily be able to own everything you dream about when your financial resources increase. The skill of feeling satisfied lies in acquiring what makes you happy within the available amount of your budget in any case.

YOUR DEBTS

12

$ You can always postpone the purchase of some necessities, no matter how important they are, and reprioritize your purchase. Your debts arise not when your needs become more than your income but when your spending is more than your budget.

$ Borrowing is one of the last resorts to address your financial problems, but it is important to pay attention so that debt does not exacerbate these problems. You must have a clear payment plan and an equally clear plan in case you fail to pay off the debt.

$ Having close people who can lend, and not being embarrassed to ask, should not encourage you to borrow frequently. Debt cannot be adopted as a continuous means of budgetary control in any case. Even debts that you trust their lenders to forgive you—if you fail to pay off—should not be counted on. You can build a stable life only on what you have of money and not on what others can help you with.

(💰) Proactive debt treatment is better than dealing with debt embarrassment and repayment problems. Be committed not to spend exceeding your income in any way, no matter what temptations or even what seems to you as necessities at times. Deduct an emergency amount as much as possible, and do not touch it for any investment, no matter how tempting. As you assess your financial situation, try to be as far-sighted as possible; it makes no sense to think of how to avoid an accident just when you are about to get into it if the accident indications seemed to you clearly from afar.

(💰) It is never the best solution to treat debts with further debts, whether from the same source or from an alternative one. This looks like an action to justify postponing thinking about radically solving the problem, which is just a manner of procrastination that exacerbates the problem.

(💰) Carefully studied loans for specific investments are not primarily debts, but poor investments management may turn the consequences of those loans into worse than the consequences of the debts arising from borrowing to pay critical or urgent necessities.

(💰) It is OK to enjoy the sweet taste of a debt that relieves you of a great distress, but at the same time, it is wise to remember the bitter taste of default when the time comes.

Regardless of the financial feasibility, it does not seem ethical to borrow because you do not want to touch your savings or other investments. However, if you feel this is necessary to you in a specific situation, it is morally important to make sure that you are approaching someone who will not be burdened by your debt.

It is not a bad idea to have a specific person whom you borrow from and who borrows from you when needed. Mutual trust will minimize the problems of misunderstanding and annoyance in cases of default by any party due to force majeure or any reason. But always remember that it is necessary not to adopt debt as a regular plan for managing your financial and life affairs in general. It is better to consider debt—in most of its forms—as the last solution that is adopted to avoid declaring bankruptcy.

Dealing with debt includes responses to borrowing requests you receive, not only your need to borrow from others. Your view and evaluation should be comprehensive for every request someone addresses to borrow from you so that the human and ethical aspects are evaluated alongside your financial capabilities. It is better that your willingness to support is not defined only by a single separate factor.

YOUR REFERENCES IN SPENDING AND SAVING **13**

Spending and saving habits are probably genetic. However, there will be models that inspire you regarding the ways of spending and methods of saving. Try to pay attention to these models and deal with them very carefully. Decisions related to money affect your life directly and seriously.

Your spending role models are just as significant as your role models in saving are. Spending and saving are two interrelated behaviors, one leading to the other in one way or another.

The challenge of dealing with money is not always to survive insolvency. Spending cheaply has damages that are often no less dangerous than the damages of extravagance.

Being inspired by any references in spending or saving does not always mean literal imitation of them. Sometimes you might need to avoid certain spending or saving approaches that are done by your references and not suiting you.

💰 While you are getting inspired by your role models in spending, do not forget to make sure that they are able to control their financial resources, or at least deal steadily with their financial crises and get out of them wisely.

💰 The most wonderful thing that your examples in spending and saving could inspire is creating additional sources of income.

💰 Your references in spending and saving constantly constitute a source of reassurance and confidence for you in one way or another. However, always try to make the final decisions in your financial dealings stem from within you, no matter how deep the inspiration you receive from others.

💰 You don't necessarily need to have constant references on spending and savings, but if you are fortunate to find such examples, be sure to draw inspiration from them as deeply as you can.

💰 Your reference in spending or saving is a significant title that you should not give to anyone just because you admire their great ability to save money or the way they spend generously on themselves or others. Your financial inspiration should give you the ability to deal with critical financial situations and their relevant consequences comprehensively and satisfactorily.

Your best spending references not only inspire you about the audacity of spending but also about its optimal forms; and your best saving references not only inspire you about the possible extents of saving but also about the ways to benefit from your saving, no matter how much you succeed to save.

TAKING RISK

14

Like anything in existence, no investment lives forever. Every project bears with its birth the seed of its annihilation, which is its life span. Be smart in estimating the life span of your investment so that you are not surprised by the end of it with your hands idle. Investments are not like humans; you should not stay with your investment until the last breath.

There is no investment that is without risk, but it is not wise to enter an investment with uncalculated risk. On the other hand, a very carefully calculated risk is no longer a risk, which most probably deprives the investment of its desired benefits.

Not moving does not mean that you are staying in the safety zone. Sticking with your current job that you've been in for so many years isn't necessarily the best option when there is already clear evidence of drastic changes that don't seem to be in your favor. On the other hand, do not rush to leave your place just because of strong recurring rumors of a change you do not like in your current job, even if many colleagues responded to those rumors by leaving for somewhere else.

💲 Great opportunities often come about because of rare luck or the courage to take risks. Even if you are stable in your work and an opportunity to move to another job emerged—not without major technical or administrative challenges but with a much higher financial return—it is worth thinking seriously and even taking practical steps for planning to move if you feel that the time for change has come and that you can, with some effort and focus, overcome the challenges of the shift.

💲 Courage to take risks does not mean deliberately looking for risks to take. A promising risk appears to you as does a bright idea suddenly appearing as inspiration that helps you reach safety on any level.

💲 Since no risk should be taken without even a little—but necessarily deep—study or reflection, the risks that you had taken or you had been earlier exposed to in any way are the best that can help you in your assessment of the risk you are currently dealing with.

💲 It's good to learn the lessons of risks others have taken in their similar or even different businesses, but it is important to note that the circumstances accompany others' experiences do not necessarily apply to you in all scenarios.

When it comes to the savings you have accumulated over the course of your career throughout your life, never risk all or most of the money. Your investments should be then very carefully considered, and it is wise to stay away as much as possible from taking any risk.

Risk does not become a risk when you have no other choice. In this case, you should study it carefully and deeply and be ready to implement your plan in case of its failure.

If, however, you decide to risk all your savings in an investment at any point in your life, you should at least make sure that whatever backup plan you have is effective in case the investment fails.

15

YOUR RETIREMENT PLAN

$ Money is an essential part of your retirement plan, but it is the nature and quality of life you look forward to after retirement that determines how much money you need then.

$ Like any investment, don't risk putting your retirement plan in one basket. Diversify your retirement investments and avoid risking them as much as you can.

$ Nowadays continuing to work for a few more years after retirement has become a popular idea as part of the retirement plan for many. It is nice that this makes you feel a little safe, but it is wise to deal more carefully with the returns of work for this period, without forgetting the need not to postpone enjoying your resources and savings until a period after which you may not be able to enjoy what you collect.

$ The retirement stage is usually accompanied by a change in the spending pattern, which is a natural change that does not have to be by reducing spending but by adjusting its direction to suit the requirements of this stage, considering the personal circumstances of each one and the cultural influences of each society. If your resources force you to reduce your spending during this stage, direct some of your spending to qualitative activities or items to make up for the quantity you missed.

It's wise to start making your retirement investment while on the job as much as you can. This will give you the opportunity to test the feasibility of this investment in a calm manner and correct its mistakes or even replace it with another investment if you find that it is not suitable.

Owning your dream house basically helps make your retirement plan more robust, but before you drain your savings in your dream house, you must make sure that you have enough to spend after you live in that house. Securing housing is mostly on the top of every person's priorities list, but one has to pay attention at least to what comes next at the top of the list.

The way you retire reflects your behavior throughout your career interval. It's important to pay attention early to your spending, saving, and investment approaches to avoid unpleasant surprises when you retire.

💲 You will be disappointed if you overestimate your postretirement plan. There is no problem with ambition, but do not base all your expectations on one or a few exceptional examples and try to study all the cases you can reach. When you decide to set your own ceiling on extraordinary challenges, you must be prepared to accept the potential consequences.

💲 The challenge is not all about money during retirement, but your preoccupation with social activities and volunteer work occupies your time, distracts you from purely consumption behavior, and reduces your anxiety about the need for money.

💲 Don't be very worried when you find that your retirement plan is not fully secured; your current job itself is not fully secured. Sometimes our obsession with insecurity is the cause of our feeling insecure more than being due to any other tangible threat.

YOUR WISH LIST

16

There is no limit to your wish list. The challenge lies in the effort that you have to make to achieve what you put on your wish list and the patience you need before you see every wish come true over the course of your life.

Your wish list is not supposed to be a burden on your budget. On the contrary, you can include in it wishes that, when achieved, will benefit you by increasing your income.

Some wishes require money to fulfill, but it is important not to limit all your wishes to what money can bring. The doors to success and satisfaction are many and accessing them is not always linked to money. In any case, regardless of money, control your wishes as much as possible, and do not let them control you.

It is a good idea to update your wish list every once in a while. Do not hesitate to delete the wishes that no longer mean much to you, and replace them with the new wishes that your ambition or desire has risen to.

(\$) Even if you view it as less important, while you are waiting for another wish on the list to come true, give the fulfilled wish a proper and deep celebration, and let it inject you with a dose of refreshing hope.

(\$) Make your wish list an opportunity to free your life from the grip of others on all levels as much as possible. Look at every wish, considering that its fulfillment is your responsibility alone and no one has any major part in that.

(\$) What you achieved of what you did not plan in advance, or even dream of, makes up for what you did not achieve within your wish list.

(\$) Your advancing age makes you calmer and more reassured about what wishes have come true and what haven't. This should not make you be less enthusiastic about wishes as you age. An important qualitative change happens to a person as they age, but wishes—meaning hope for life—must not stop regardless of the nature of the wishes.

(\$) It would seem strange to finish fulfilling every wish on your wish list. Then you may feel great satisfaction or, conversely, a sense of anxiety because you have nothing to look forward to. When you meditate deeply, you will discover that you have many wishes that you are looking forward to fulfilling, but you just haven't taken a pause to update your wish list.

Make a separate list, and write down what great and beautiful things happen to you without you planning it or even thinking about it. Celebrate deeply what you put on this list being precious gifts of fate that you would never have counted.

WHAT DOES A BLESSING MEAN?

17

- The blessing in money is not a fantasy; it is simply your deep conviction that you can manage your affairs with the money available with you, regardless of whether it is a little or a lot.

- Like happiness, a money blessing will not fall on you from heaven. You have to believe deeply in it to get it.

- The blessing in money is not the result of waiting for the outcome of a negative feeling of helplessness and inaction. On the contrary, it is the fruit of a positive feeling of an optimal balance between your ambition and your conviction of what is in your hands at any moment.

- Even if you do not believe in what is intangible, spending for charitable deeds deepens the feeling of the blessing of money as it rids you of the obsession with thrift.

- Feeling the blessing in money does not mean that you expect sudden increases in your balance from time to time but that you do not feel that you are poor even when your balance decreases due to spending for this reason or that.

The blessings in money are ideation splendors shining to guide you to the possibilities of moving comfortably within the range of financial resources at your disposal.

The blessing in money is a deep concept that requires a pure spirit to feel it. It is not wise to raid a person who is complaining of a severe financial crisis and try to persuade them to sense the blessing in money before you guide them on the way to escape from their financial hardships.

The blessings in money cannot be reached by any question that begins with "How much … ?" They are answers that leak to you spontaneously as you contemplate confidently about how you should enjoy the little amount of money available with you.

The blessing in money is never related to the money in itself but to the aspects of its spending and your feeling of satisfaction with what the money goes for.

The blessing in money seems to be primarily about spending more than it is about saving.

18

MONEY AND HAPPINESS

$ The happiness that money brings for people is basically for two contradictory reasons: either spending or saving. Look for the way that makes you happy in dealing with money, and do not exaggerate whatever way you choose.

$ The way we deal with money is actually more of our destiny than it is our choice. Do not be ashamed of your destiny, and face the challenges that lie in it patiently so that you can feel the greatest degree of peace and happiness.

$ Money will not be even just a means to happiness if you think that all your happiness lies in it.

$ The secret of happiness is greater and more complex than placing its responsibility on money alone.

$ It's not fair to blame our unhappiness on money while it didn't even claim that it would make us happy.

Happiness with an abundance of money is a more difficult challenge than happiness with its scarcity; at least in the latter case one wishes oneself to seize happiness when one's financial condition improves.

Money can indeed be a powerful cause of happiness if we realize that what we truly need is the amount that meets our basic requirements or a little more and absolutely not great wealth.

One of the greatest challenges of happiness with money is that the more money we have, the more we need and spend, so much of what we used to consider luxury become some of our basic needs.

The magic of money in achieving happiness lies in the fact that money is the means by which one can possess materials and even fulfill many emotional wishes. But it should be noted that the acquisition of any material and the fulfillment of any wish, no matter how expensive and valuable, are only means to feel happiness for a limited period and not the ultimate happiness.

Away from money specifically, eternal happiness is an illusion humans insist on believing is reality and chasing it.

Printed in the United States
by Baker & Taylor Publisher Services